ARBOR DAY

A CROWELL HOLIDAY BOOK

ARBOR DAY

By Aileen Fisher

Illustrations by

Nonny Hogrogian

Thomas Y. Crowell Company

New York

 Manufactured in the United States of America / Library of Congress Catalog Card No. 65-10751

1 2 3 4 5 6 7 8 9 10

Crowell Holiday Books

Edited by Susan Bartlett Weber

ST. VALENTINE'S DAY

PASSOVER

ARBOR DAY

FLAG DAY

MOTHER'S DAY

Arbor Day is a day for trees.

It is a day to think about trees and soil and wind and rain.

And it is a day to think about America.

It is a day to think about:

What became of the great forests that used to grow in our country?

Why does America need trees?

How can we help to keep America beautiful?

In the early days of our country, settlers looked at the great forests of America and sighed.
The trees were in the way.
They grew to the edge of the sea.
They covered the valleys, they covered the hills.

The settlers needed room for their homes and fields.
And so they began to chop.
Axes rang out in the forests.
Trees creaked, and crashed to the ground.
Oxen pulled away the logs.

But the settlers did not cut all the trees.
Their fields were small.
They left many trees standing for shade and beauty.
They left wood and lumber for another day.

Then the lumbermen came.
They looked at the forests and smiled.
The trees would put money in their pockets.

Chop! Chop!

Crash! Crash!

The lumbermen cut down whole forests of trees.

They floated the logs down the rivers.

They built sawmills, and sold lumber.

They made money.

But they did not think about keeping America beautiful.

They left stumps and ugly piles of brush behind them.

They left danger behind them.

The brush easily caught fire, and fires roared through the cut-over land.

The lumbermen did not think about saving America's soil. Neither did many of the settlers.

They did not think about roots of trees holding the soil in place.

They did not think about the green roof of leaves breaking the force of the rain.

When they cut down the forests, the green roof of leaves was gone.

The tree roots died.

Rain pounded down on the cut-over hill-sides, and soil washed away from the dead roots.

The hillsides became waste land where nothing would grow.

All this time settlers were moving west-
ward.
They reached the prairies and the plains,
and stared at what they saw.

A sea of green and gold spread around them.

A sea of grass!

There were no trees to cut.

There were no trees anywhere, except along
the streams.

This time the settlers did not have to clear
the land to make room for their homes
and crops.
They plowed up the sod.
They cut strips of sod to build sod houses.
They plowed up more and more ground.

Then the wind began to blow.

It raced across the sea of gold and green.
It reached the plowed ground.
It whirled the loose soil into the air and blew it away.

There was nothing on the plains to break
the force of the wind.
There was nothing to keep the wind from
blowing away the loose plowed
ground.

In Nebraska a man stood in his field and
watched the wind.
His name was J. Sterling Morton.
His hobby was trees, and his head was full
of thoughts.

He thought:

Trees are beautiful. And they are useful.
Trees make green walls in a flat country like Nebraska.
The walls break the force of the wind and keep it from blowing away the soil.
Fallen leaves hold moisture in the ground.
Nebraska needs trees.

He thought:

Treetops make green roofs for the hillsides of America.
Leaves break the force of the rain and keep it from washing away the soil.
America needs trees.

Then Mr. Morton had an idea.

He began to talk and write about trees.
He said we must plant, plant, plant.
He said we must set aside a special day for trees.
He called that special day Arbor Day.

Of course, Mr. Morton knew that planting trees was not a new idea.
It was a very old idea.
For thousands of years farmers all over the world had planted fruit trees, nut trees, olive trees, and shade trees.

The Aztec Indians planted a tree each time a child was born, and they gave the tree and the child the same name.

A man called Johnny Appleseed spent his life planting apple trees in Ohio and Indiana and Kentucky.

But part of Mr. Morton's idea was new.
He wanted a special day each year for planting trees.
He wanted a great many people to plant a great many trees on that special day.
No one else had thought of that.

The first Arbor Day came in Nebraska in
April, 1872.

The people were eager to make their state
beautiful.

They wanted to save the soil.

And so they planted trees, and more trees.

They planted a million trees on that first
Arbor Day.

The news raced across the country like the
prairie wind.
Other states began to set aside a special day
for trees.

Now Arbor Day comes once a year throughout America, when the weather is good for planting.

In the north it comes in April or May.

In the south it usually comes in January or February.

On Arbor Day boys and girls put on plays
and programs in school.
They sing songs about trees and about
America the beautiful.

They talk about trees making cool shadows under the bright sky, and bringing a breath of the country into the city.

And they help to plant trees.

Sometimes they talk about birds, too.

Trees need birds to protect them from insects.

Birds need trees to protect them from enemies and weather.

That is why Arbor Day and Bird Day come at the same time in some states.

On Arbor Day boys and girls all over
America think about trees.
They think about the trees of yesterday.
They think about the trees of today.
But most of all they think about trees for
tomorrow.

ABOUT THE AUTHOR

Aileen Fisher has spent most of her life in close touch with the endless fascinations of nature. Growing up on a farm near Iron River in Michigan's Upper Peninsula, with an older brother and two younger sisters, she early learned the joys of country living. Wildlife roamed the woods along the river; in the barnyard were horses, cows, chickens, rabbits, pigs, cats, dogs, and even a stray lamb raised on a bottle. Miss Fisher now lives on a 200-acre ranch in the foothills of the Rocky Mountains.

She attended the University of Chicago and received a degree in journalism from the University of Missouri. After working in Chicago for a few years, she moved to her ranch near Boulder, Colorado, where she writes her delightful books for children.

ABOUT THE ILLUSTRATOR

Nonny Hogrogian is a native New Yorker. She was graduated from Hunter College, and has studied at the Art Students League and with Antonio Frasconi and Hodaka Yoshida. Miss Hogrogian is engaged professionally in the design, illustration, and publishing of books. She has traveled throughout the United States and in Canada and the West Indies.